TRAEGER GRILLS & SMOKER COOKBOOK:

THE COMPLETE GUIDE TO MASTER YOUR WOOD PELLET GRILL

Peter Burns

D1728109

Sommario

Introduction

Trager is a grill and smoker-manufacturing company that is based in Oregon and reputed for using all-natural flavored wood pellets. As far as its origins, Joe Traeger wanted to cook a scrumptious meal for his family when he discovered that his gas grill was burned down.

The very next day, he decided to make a grill with wooden pellets to ensure a fire-free barbeque for the entire summer. As time passed, the first grill by Traeger was mass-produced in 1988.

Subsequently, the company released six different models of barbeque grills, apart from rubs, sauces, spices, smokers, and even apparel. Until 2005, Traeger Grills owned the wood pellet stove patent.

So, how does the Traeger grill work? When you turn the appliance on, the motor starts the rotation of a screw-like device, called the auger, which feeds the burn pot. The pellets then are ignited, and exhaust is via the chimney.

Traeger grills are also fitted with air convection that feeds air to the burning pellets. This ensures that the heat is efficiently distributed, and the air around the food is filled with smoke. Similar to a convection oven, the heat is moved around the meat.

Some special aspects of the Traeger Grills are:

1. The fuel

Most other types of grills make use of charcoal, natural gas, or propane as a source of fuel. In the case of these fuel sources, the user needs to have a bit of knowledge of the grill type and be present to 'babysit' the grill.

On the other hand, Traeger grills use wood pellets that are all-natural and all-wood. These pellets can burn well in a controlled environment and provide flavorful food. Additionally, these pellets are FDA-approved and safe for home and outdoor uses.

The pellets are available in 14 distinct flavors. They can be used to create a new range of individual flavors and do not harm the environment when burned.

2. Flavor

Traeger pellets are available in 14 different types of pellets like pecan, apple, mesquite, hickory, etc. Apart from infusing delicious flavor to the meat, you can also use them for baking sweets like pie and cookies.

3. No flare-up

There are no flare-ups in roasting, baking, smoking, or grilling when you are using indirect electric heat, not gas. This is because electric heat (indirect) does not lead to flare-ups. The appliances are also not exposed to dripping temperatures.

4. Control of the temperature

One of the best aspects of the Traeger Grill is total control of the temperature. Once you set it, the grill is capable of maintaining consistent heat, even if the weather may not look favorable.

The Traeger grills can be set in 5-degree increments, which is a feature not seen in many grills, especially charcoal and gas ones. All you need to do is cook the food using the recipe and not worry about the appliance dropping down the temperature.

Additionally, since pellets are essentially electric, you are not tied to your grill like a gas grill. For instance, you do not have to keep checking the grill from time-to-time to ensure that the food has not burned.

5. Environmentally-friendly

Grills manufactured by Traeger make use of all-natural and real wood pellets that can burn within a controlled system, thereby offering flavor, ease of use, and convenience.

These grills are also approved by the FDA, and the flavors of the pellets can be blended to create a mix of flavors. Additionally, burning these pellets will not cause any harm to the environment, as mentioned before.

Tips and Tricks for Using Your Traeger Grill

If you are looking for some tips and tricks that can help you better utilize your Traeger grill, they are listed for you. If you already have the appliance, you are already on the sweet side of life. Whether you are a grill newbie or a master, there are always things that you can learn to become the ultimate grill and smoker master.

Some of the top tricks, tips, and hacks that can make your barbequing, smoking, and grilling experience better include:

1. Always use disposable drip bucket liners

If you get tired of cleaning up that slimy residue every time you decide to grill or smoke some steak or are prone to bumping the bucket off accidentally when putting on the cover, it is recommended that you look for bucket liners - disposable ones, of course. With the help of these disposable drip bucket liners, cleaning will become much easier.

2. Grill lights to light the way

If you plan on cooking at night or are always bumping around the grill in the dark, you can look for some grill lights. If you are a serious smoker but are busy dealing with the headlamp or flashlight, these grill lights will come in very handy.

No wonder this device is one of the top-sellers on several online shopping sites. The grill lights are fitted with a magnetic base and can clamp and bend according to the shape of the grill.

3. Drip tray liners for easier cleaning

If you want to get serious, then it is time to dump the aluminum foil. Once you have the drip tray liners, you will not have to deal with wadded up, oily, blackened, or small tears in the foil.

The overall idea here is to make the cleaning process easier so that you can redirect your focus on the more important things, such as smoking and grilling.

4. Meat temperature and meat smoking magnets to measure the temperature accurately

One of the worst things that can happen while grilling and smoking meat is guessing the cooking temperature. With the help of meat smoking and temperature magnets, you can now leave all the frantic web searches behind.

With these devices, you will know the internal temperature that you need to cook meat safely. Then, you will always have perfectly cooked pieces of meat all the time.

5. Wireless thermometer or Tappecue for the perfect temperature

You have already spent hundreds of dollars on a perfect grill. However, you can still end up spending tens and thousands of dollars more each time you decide to cook on it.

If you want to protect your important investment from harm, you need to ensure that you do not have to 'peek' while cooking. With the Tappecue, you will get the internal temperature that you are looking for.

6. Swap out pellets with bucket head vacuum

Imagine that you need to move from the apple to the hickory flavor. However, you see that the grill is more than half-full of apple pellets. What can you do in this scenario? Of course, you can choose to wait until the pellets cool down and then remove them. Another solution to this issue is using a bucket head vacuum.

Get the appropriate bucket head for a 5-gallon bucket and simply vacuum out the pellets. Once done, you will be left with storage that you can use at any time. Additionally, you do not even need a specialized bucket for this purpose; you can use a simple bucket and storage lid kit that is fitted with a filter.

7. Add extra smoke on any type of cooking with an A-maze-n Smoker Tube

If you love smoking, you should definitely buy a dedicated smoker tube – like the A-maze-n Smoker Tube. Known for its great simplicity, this tube is one of the best tools for a seasoned smoker. All you need to do is to add some pellets and light them at just one end. Then, leave it on the grates.

A smoker tube is a great option for cold smoking fish, nuts, and cheese; of course, it can also be used for some extra smoke on meats, like brisket, pulled pork, etc.

Chapter 1.   Beef recipe

1 Smoked Trip Tip with Java Chophouse

Preparation Time: 10 Minutes

Cooking Time: 90 Minutes

Servings: 4

Ingredients:

- 2 tbsp olive oil

- 2 tbsp java chophouse seasoning

- 3 lb. trip tip roast, fat cap, and silver skin removed

Directions:

1. Startup your wood pellet grill and smoker and set the temperature to 225°F.

2. Rub the roast with olive oil and seasoning, then place it on the smoker rack.

3. Smoke until the internal temperature is 140°F.

4. Remove the tri-tip from the smoker and let rest for 10 minutes before serving. Enjoy.

Nutrition:

Calories 270

Total fat 7g

Total Carbs 0g

Protein 23g

Sodium: 47mg

Potassium 289mg

Preparation Time: 5 Minutes

Cooking Time: 3 Hours

Servings: 7

Ingredients:

- 3-1/2 beef top round
- 3 tbsp vegetable oil
- Prime rib rub
- 2 cups beef broth
- One russet potato, peeled and sliced
- Two carrots, peeled and sliced
- Two celery stalks, chopped
- One onion, sliced
- Two thyme sprigs

Directions:

1. Rub the roast with vegetable oil and place it on the roasting fat side up. Season with prime rib rub, then pours the beef broth.

2. Set the temperature to 500°F and preheat the wood pellet grill for 15 minutes with the lid closed.

3. Cook for 30 minutes or until the roast is well seared.

4. Reduce temperature to 225°F. Add the veggies and thyme and cover with foil. Cook for three more hours or until the internal temperature reaches 135°F.

5. Remove from the grill and let rest for 10 minutes. Slice against the grain and serve with vegetables and the pan drippings.

6. Enjoy.

Nutrition:

Calories 697

Total fat 10g

Total Carbs 127g

Protein 34g

Sugar 14g

Fiber 22g

Sodium: 3466mg

Potassium 2329mg

3 Wood Pellet Grill Deli-Style Roast Beef

Preparation Time: 15 Minutes

Cooking Time: 4 Hours

Servings: 2

Ingredients:

- 4lb round-bottomed roast
- 1 tbsp coconut oil
- 1/4 tbsp garlic powder
- 1/4 tbsp onion powder
- 1/4 tbsp thyme
- 1/4 tbsp oregano
- 1/2 tbsp paprika
- 1/2 tbsp salt
- 1/2 tbsp black pepper

Directions:

1. Combine all the dry hubs to get a dry rub.

2. Roll the roast in oil, then coat with the rub.

3. Set your grill to 185°F and place the roast on the grill.

4. Smoke for 4 hours or until the internal temperature reaches 140°F.

5. Remove the roast from the grill and let rest for 10 minutes.

6. Slice thinly and serve.

Nutrition:

Calories 90

Total fat 3g

Total Carbs 0g

Protein 14g

Sodium: 420mg

4 Bacon-Swiss Cheesesteak Meatloaf

Preparation Time: 15 minutes

Cooking Time: 2 hours

Servings: 8-10

Ingredients:

- 1 tablespoon canola oil

- 2 garlic cloves, finely chopped

- 1 medium onion, finely chopped

- 1 poblano chile, stemmed, seeded, and finely chopped

- 2 pounds extra-lean ground beef

- 2 tablespoons Montreal steak seasoning

- 1 tablespoon A.1. Steak Sauce

- ½ pound bacon, cooked and crumbled

- 2 cups shredded Swiss cheese

- 1 egg, beaten

- 2 cups breadcrumbs

- ½ cup Tiger Sauce

Directions:

1. On your stove top, heat the canola oil in a medium sauté pan over medium-high heat. Add the garlic, onion, and poblano, and sauté for 3 to 5 minutes, or until the onion is just barely translucent.

2. Supply your smoker with wood pellets and follow the manufacturer's specific start-up procedure. Preheat, with the lid closed, to 225°F.

3. In a large bowl, combine the sautéed vegetables, ground beef, steak seasoning, steak sauce,

bacon, Swiss cheese, egg, and breadcrumbs. Mix with your hands until well incorporated, then shape into a loaf.

4.   Put the meatloaf in a cast iron skillet and place it on the grill. Insert meat thermometer inserted in the loaf reads 165°F.

5.   Top with the meatloaf with the Tiger Sauce, remove from the grill, and let rest for about 10 minutes before serving.

Nutrition:

Calories: 120 Cal

Fat: 2 g

Carbohydrates: 0 g

Protein: 23 g

Fiber: 0 g

Preparation Time: 20 minutes

Cooking Time: 12-16 minutes

Servings: 3-4

Ingredients:

- 1 (1½- to 2-pound) London broil or top round steak
- ¼ cup soy sauce
- 2 tablespoons white wine
- 2 tablespoons extra-virgin olive oil
- ¼ cup chopped scallions
- 2 tablespoons packed brown sugar
- 2 garlic cloves, minced
- 2 teaspoons red pepper flakes
- 1 teaspoon freshly ground black pepper

Directions:

1. Using a meat mallet, pound the steak lightly all over on both sides to break down its fibers and tenderize. You are not trying to pound down the thickness.

2. In a medium bowl, make the marinade by combining the soy sauce, white wine, olive oil, scallions, brown sugar, garlic, red pepper flakes, and black pepper.

3. Put the steak in a shallow plastic container with a lid and pour the marinade over the meat. Cover and refrigerate for 4 hours.

4. Supply your smoker with wood pellets and follow the manufacturer's specific start-up

procedure. Preheat, with the lid closed, to 350°F.

5. Place the steak directly on the grill, close the lid, and smoke for 6 minutes. Flip, then smoke with the lid closed for 6 to 10 minutes more, or until a meat thermometer inserted in the meat reads 130°F for medium-rare.

6. The meat's temperature will rise by about 5 degrees while it rests.

Nutrition:

Calories: 316 Cal

Fat: 3 g

Carbohydrates: 0 g

Protein: 54 g

Fiber: 0 g

6 French Onion Burgers

Preparation Time: 35 minutes

Cooking Time: 20-25 minutes

Servings: 4

Ingredients:

- 1-pound lean ground beef
- 1 tablespoon minced garlic
- 1 teaspoon Better Than Bouillon Beef Base
- 1 teaspoon dried chives
- 1 teaspoon freshly ground black pepper
- 8 slices Gruyère cheese, divided
- ½ cup soy sauce
- 1 tablespoon extra-virgin olive oil
- 1 teaspoon liquid smoke

- 3 medium onions, cut into thick slices (do not separate the rings)

- 1 loaf French bread, cut into 8 slices

- 4 slices provolone cheese

Directions:

1. In a large bowl, mix together the ground beef, minced garlic, beef base, chives, and pepper until well blended.

2. Divide the meat mixture and shape into 8 thin burger patties.

3. Top each of 4 patties with one slice of Gruyère, then top with the remaining 4 patties to create 4 stuffed burgers.

4. Supply your smoker with wood pellets and follow the manufacturer's specific start-up

procedure. Preheat, with the lid closed, to 425°F.

5. Arrange the burgers directly on one side of the grill, close the lid, and smoke for 10 minutes. Flip and smoke with the lid closed for 10 to 15 minutes more, or until a meat thermometer inserted in the burgers reads 160°F. Add another Gruyère slice to the burgers during the last 5 minutes of smoking to melt.

6. Meanwhile, in a small bowl, combine the soy sauce, olive oil, and liquid smoke.

7. Arrange the onion slices on the grill and paste on both sides with the soy sauce mixture. Smoke with the lid closed for 20

minutes, flipping halfway through.

8. Lightly toast the French bread slices on the grill. Layer each of 4 slices with a burger patty, a slice of provolone cheese, and some of the smoked onions. Top each with another slice of toasted French bread. Serve immediately.

Nutrition:

Calories: 704 Cal

Fat: 43 g

Carbohydrates: 28 g

Protein: 49 g

Fiber: 2 g

Chapter 2. Pork recipe

7   Classic Pulled Pork

Preparation Time: 15 minutes

Cooking Time: 16-20 hours

Servings: 8-12

Ingredients:

- 1 (6- to 8-pound) bone-in pork shoulder

- 2 tablespoons yellow mustard

- 1 batch Not-Just-for-Pork Rub

Directions:

1. Supply your smoker with wood pellets and follow the manufacturer's specific start-up procedure.

2. Coat the pork shoulder all over with mustard and season it with the rub.

3. Place the shoulder on the grill grate and smoke until its internal temperature reaches 195°F.

4. Pull the shoulder from the grill and wrap it completely in aluminum foil or butcher paper. Place it in a cooler, cover the cooler, and let it rest for 1 or 2 hours.

5. Remove the pork shoulder from the cooler and unwrap it. Remove the shoulder bone and pull the pork apart using just your fingers. Serve immediately as desired. Leftovers are encouraged.

Nutrition:

Calories: 414 Cal

Fat: 29 g

Carbohydrates: 1 g

Protein: 38 g

Fiber: 0 g

Preparation Time: 15 minutes

Cooking Time: 16-20 hours

Servings: 8-12

Ingredients:

- 1 (6- to 8-pound) bone-in pork shoulder

- 2 cups Tea Injectable made with Not-Just-for-Pork Rub

- 2 tablespoons yellow mustard

- 1 batch Not-Just-for-Pork Rub

Directions:

1. Supply your smoker with wood pellets and follow the manufacturer's specific start-up procedure.

2. Inject the pork shoulder throughout with the tea injectable.

3. Coat the pork shoulder all over with mustard and season it with the rub. Work rub onto

4. Place the shoulder directly on the grill grate and smoke until its internal temperature reaches 160°F and a dark bark has formed on the exterior.

5. Pull the shoulder from the grill and wrap it completely in aluminum foil or butcher paper.

6. Increase the grill's temperature to 350°F.

7. Return the pork shoulder to the grill and cook until its internal temperature reaches 195°F.

8.   Pull the shoulder from the grill and place it in a cooler. Cover the cooler and let the pork rest for 1 or 2 hours.

9.   Remove the pork shoulder from the cooler and unwrap it. Remove the shoulder bone and pull the pork apart using just your fingers. Serve immediately.

Nutrition:

Calories: 257 Cal

Fat: 15 g

Carbohydrates: 0 g

Protein: 29 g

Fiber: 0 g

Preparation Time: 10 minutes

Cooking Time: 55 minutes

Servings: 4

Ingredients:

- 4 (8-ounce) pork chops, bone-in or boneless (I use boneless)

- Salt

- Freshly ground black pepper

Directions:

1. Supply your smoker with wood pellets and follow the manufacturer's specific start-up procedure.

2. Drizzle pork chop with salt and pepper to season.

3. Place the chops directly on the grill grate and smoke for 30 minutes.

4. Increase the grill's temperature to 350°F. Continue to cook the chops until their internal temperature reaches 145°F.

5. Remove the pork chops from the grill and let them rest for 5 minutes before serving.

Nutrition:

Calories: 130 Cal

Fat: 12 g

Carbohydrates: 3 g

Protein: 20 g

Fiber: 0 g

Preparation Time: 15 minutes

Cooking Time: 4-5 hours

Servings: 4-6

Ingredients:

2 (1-pound) pork tenderloins

1 batch Not-Just-for-Pork Rub

Directions:

Supply your smoker with wood pellets and follow the manufacturer's specific start-up procedure. Preheat the grill

Generously season the tenderloins with the rub. W

Put tenderloins on the grill and smoke for 4 or 5 hours, until their internal temperature reaches 145°F.

The tenderloins must be put out of the grill and let it rest for 5-10 minutes then begin slicing into thin pieces before serving

Nutrition:

Calories: 180 Cal

Fat: 8 g

Carbohydrates: 3 g

Protein: 24 g

Fiber: 0 g

11 Teriyaki Pork Tenderloin

Preparation Time: 30 minutes

Cooking Time: 1 ½ hours to 2 hours

Servings: 4-6

Ingredients:

- 2 (1-pound) pork tenderloins

- 1 batch Easy Teriyaki Marinade

- Smoked salt

Directions:

1. In a large zip-top bag, combine the tenderloins and marinade. Seal the bag, turn to coat, and refrigerate the pork for at least 30 minutes—I recommend up to overnight.

2. Supply your smoker with wood pellets and follow the manufacturer's specific start-up

procedure. Preheat the grill, with the lid closed, to 180°F.

3. As you get the tenderloins from the marinade begin seasoning them with smoked salt

4. Place the tenderloins directly on the grill grate and smoke for 1 hour.

5. Increase the grill's temperature to 300°F and continue to cook until the pork's internal temperature reaches 145°F.

6. With the tenderloins removed from the grill, let it cool for at least 5-10 minutes before slicing and serving

Nutrition:

Calories: 110 Cal

Fat: 3 g

Carbohydrates: 2 g

Protein: 18 g

Fiber: 0 g

12 Barbecued Tenderloin

Preparation Time: 5 minutes

Cooking Time: 3o minutes

Servings: 4-6

Ingredients:

- 2 (1-pound) pork tenderloins

- 1 batch Sweet and Spicy Cinnamon Rub

Directions:

1. Supply your smoker with wood pellets and follow the manufacturer's specific start-up procedure. Preheat the grill

2. Generously season the tenderloins with the rub. Work rubs onto meat.

3. Place the tenderloins and smoke internal temperature reaches 145°F.

4. As you put out the tenderloins from the grill, let it cool down for 5-10 minutes before slicing it up and serving it

Nutrition:

Calories: 186 Cal

Fat: 4 g

Carbohydrates: 8 g

Protein: 29 g

Fiber: 1 g

13 Smoked Avocado Pork Ribs

Preparation Time: 20 Minutes

Cooking Time: 3 Hours

Servings: 5

Ingredients:

- 2 lbs. of pork spare ribs

- 1 cup of avocado oil

- One teaspoon of garlic powder

- One teaspoon of onion powder

- One teaspoon of sweet pepper flakes

- Salt and pepper, to taste

Directions:

1. In a bowl, combine the avocado oil, garlic salt, garlic powder, onion powder, sweet pepper flakes, and salt and pepper.

2. Place pork chops in a shallow container and pour evenly avocado mixture.

3. Cover and refrigerate for at least 4 hours or overnight.

4. Start pellet grill on, lid open until the fire is established (4-5 minutes).

5. Increase the temperature to 225 and pre-heat for 10 - 15 minutes.

6. Arrange pork chops on the grill rack and smoke for 3 to 4 hours.

7. Transfer pork chops on serving plate, let them rest for 15 minutes, and serve.

Nutrition:

Calories: 677 call

Carbohydrates: 0.9g

Fat: 64g

Fiber: 0.14g

Protein: 28.2g

14 Smoked Honey - Garlic Pork Chops

Preparation Time: 15 Minutes

Cooking Time: 60 Minutes

Servings: 4

Ingredients:

- 1/4 cup of lemon juice freshly squeezed
- 1/4 cup honey (preferably a darker honey)
- Three cloves garlic, minced
- Two tablespoons of soy sauce (or tamari sauce)
- Salt and pepper to taste
- 24 ounces center-cut pork chops boneless

Directions:

1. Combine honey, lemon juice, soy sauce, garlic, and salt and pepper in a bowl.

2. Place pork in a container and pour marinade over pork.

3. Cover and marinate in a fridge overnight.

4. Remove pork from marinade and pat dry on kitchen paper towel. (Reserve marinade)

5. Start your pellet on Smoke with the lid open until the fire is established (4 - 5 minutes).

6. Increase temperature to 450 and preheat, lid closed, for 10 - 15 minutes.

7. Arrange the pork chops on the grill racks and smoke for about one hour (depending on the thickness)

8. In the meantime, heat the remaining marinade in a small saucepan over medium heat to simmer.

9. Transfer pork chops on a serving plate, pour with the marinade, and serve hot.

Nutrition:

Calories: 301.5 call

Carbohydrates: 17g

Fat: 6.5g

Fiber: 0.2g

Protein: 41g

Chapter 3. Lamb recipe

15 Grilled Lamb Sandwiches

Preparation Time: 5 minutes

Cooking Time: 50 minutes

Servings: 6

Ingredients:

- 1 (4 pounds) boneless lamb.

- 1 cup of raspberry vinegar.

- 2 tablespoons of olive oil.

- 1 tablespoon of chopped fresh thyme.

- 2 pressed garlic cloves.

- 1/4 teaspoon of salt to taste.

- 1/4 teaspoon of ground pepper.

- Sliced bread.

Directions:

1. Using a large mixing bowl, add in the raspberry vinegar, oil, and

thyme then mix properly to combine. Add in the lamb, toss to combine then let it sit in the refrigerator for about eight hours or overnight.

2.   Next, discard the marinade the season the lamb with salt and pepper to taste. Preheat a Wood Pellet Smoker and grill t0 400-500 degrees F, add in the seasoned lamb and grill for about thirty to forty minutes until it attains a temperature of 150 degrees F.

3.   Once cooked, let the lamb cool for a few minutes, slice as desired then serve on the bread with your favorite topping.

Nutrition:

Calories: 407 Cal

Fat: 23 g

Carbohydrates: 26 g

Protein: 72 g

Fiber: 2.3 g

16 Lamb Chops

Preparation Time: 10 minutes

Cooking Time: 12 minutes

Servings: 6

Ingredients:

- 6 (6-ounce) lamb chops

- 3 tablespoons olive oil

- Ground black pepper

Directions:

1. Preheat the pallet grill to 450 degrees F.

2. Coat the lamb chops with oil and then, season with salt and black pepper evenly.

3. Arrange the chops in pallet grill grate and cook for about 4-6 minutes per side.

Nutrition:

Calories: 376 Cal

Fat: 19.5 g

Carbohydrates: 0 g

Protein: 47.8 g

Fiber: 0 g

Preparation Time: 10 minutes

Cooking Time: 2 hours

Servings: 2

Ingredients:

- 2 tablespoons fresh sage
- 2 tablespoons fresh rosemary
- 2 tablespoons fresh thyme
- 2 peeled garlic cloves
- 1 tablespoon honey
- Black pepper
- ¼ cup olive oil
- 1 (1½-pound) trimmed rack lamb ribs

Directions:

1. Combine all ingredients

2. While motor is running, slowly add oil and pulse till a smooth paste is formed.

3. Coat the rib rack with paste generously and refrigerate for about 2 hours.

4. Preheat the pallet grill to 225 degrees F.

5. Arrange the rib rack in pallet grill and cook for about 2 hours.

6. Remove the rib rack from pallet grill and transfer onto a cutting board for about 10-15 minutes before slicing.

7. With a sharp knife, cut the rib rack into equal sized individual ribs and serve.

Nutrition:

Calories: 826 Cal

Fat: 44.1 g

Carbohydrates: 5.4 g

Protein: 96.3 g

Fiber: 1 g

Preparation Time: 10 minutes

Cooking Time: 4 hours

Servings: 6

Ingredients:

- 8-ounce red wine
- 2-ounce whiskey
- 2 tablespoons minced fresh rosemary
- 1 tablespoon minced garlic
- Black pepper
- 6 (1¼-pound) lamb shanks

Directions:

1. In a bowl, add all ingredients except lamb shank and mix till well combined.

2. In a large resealable bag, add marinade and lamb shank.

3. Seal the bag and shake to coat completely.

4. Refrigerate for about 24 hours.

5. Preheat the pallet grill to 225 degrees F.

6. Arrange the leg of lamb in pallet grill and cook for about 4 hours.

Nutrition:

Calories: 1507 Cal

Fat: 62 g

Carbohydrates: 68.7 g

Protein:163.3 g

Fiber: 6 g

Preparation Time: 10 minutes

Cooking Time: 2 hours and 30 minutes

Servings: 10

Ingredients:

- 1 (8-ounce) package softened cream cheese

- ¼ cup cooked and crumbled bacon

- 1 seeded and chopped jalapeño pepper

- 1 tablespoon crushed dried rosemary

- 2 teaspoons garlic powder

- 1 teaspoon onion powder

- 1 teaspoon paprika

- 1 teaspoon cayenne pepper

- Salt, to taste

- 1 (4-5-pound) butterflied leg of lamb

- 2-3 tablespoons olive oil

Directions:

1. For filling in a bowl, add all ingredients and mix till well combined.

2. For spice mixture in another small bowl, mix together all ingredients.

3. Place the leg of lamb onto a smooth surface. Sprinkle the inside of leg with some spice mixture.

4. Place filling mixture over the inside surface evenly. Roll the leg of lamb tightly and with a butcher's twine, tie the roll to secure the filling

5. Coat the outer side of roll with olive oil evenly and then sprinkle with spice mixture.

6. Preheat the pallet grill to 225-240 degrees F.

7. Arrange the leg of lamb in pallet grill and cook for about 2-2½ hours. Remove the leg of lamb from pallet grill and transfer onto a cutting board.

8. With a piece of foil, cover leg loosely and transfer onto a cutting board for about 20-25 minutes before slicing.

9. With a sharp knife, cut the leg of lamb in desired sized slices and serve.

Nutrition:

Calories: 715 Cal

Fat: 38.9 g

Carbohydrates: 2.2 g

Protein: 84.6 g

Fiber: 0.1 g

Preparation Time: 10 minutes

Cooking Time: 2 hours and 40 minutes

Servings: 2

Ingredients:

- 1 (2-pound) trimmed bone-in lamb breast
- ½ cup white vinegar
- ¼ cup yellow mustard
- ½ cup BBQ rub

Directions:

1. Preheat the pallet grill to 225 degrees F.

2. Rinse the lamb breast with vinegar evenly.

3. Coat lamb breast with mustard and the, season with BBQ rub evenly.

4. Arrange lamb breast in pallet grill and cook for about 2-2½ hours.

5. Remove the lamb breast from the pallet grill and transfer onto a cutting board for about 10 minutes before slicing.

6. With a sharp knife, cut the lamb breast in desired sized slices and serve.

Nutrition:

Calories: 877 Cal

Fat: 34.5 g

Carbohydrates: 2.2 g

Protein: 128.7 g

Fiber: 0 g

Preparation Time: 4 hours

Cooking Time: 25-30 minutes

Servings: 4

Ingredients:

- 4 lamb shoulder chops
- 4 cups buttermilk
- 1 cup cold water
- ¼ cup kosher salt
- 2 tablespoons olive oil
- 1 tablespoon Texas style rub

Directions:

1. In a large bowl, add buttermilk, water and salt and stir till salt is dissolved.

2. Add chops and coat with mixture evenly.

3. Refrigerate for at least 4 hours. Remove the chops from bowl and rinse under cold water.

4. Coat the chops with olive oil and then sprinkle with rub evenly. Preheat the pallet grill to 240 degrees F.

5. Arrange the chops in pallet grill grate and cook for about 25-30 minute or till desired doneness.

6. Meanwhile preheat the broiler of oven.

7. Cook the chops under broiler till browned.

Nutrition:

Calories: 328 Cal

Fat: 18.2 g

Carbohydrates:11.7 g

Protein: 30.1 g

Fiber: 0 g

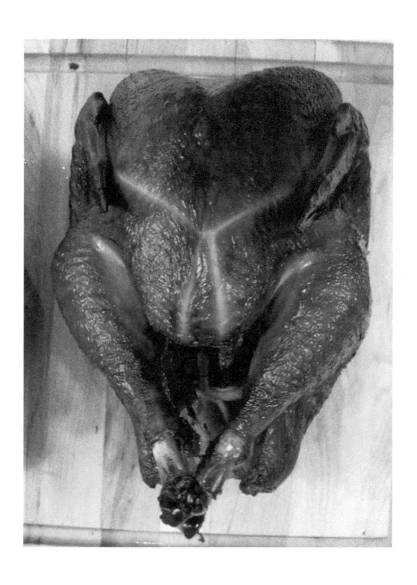

Chapter 4. Poultry recipe

Preparation Time: 25 minutes

Cooking Time: 30 minutes

Servings: 6

Ingredients:

- 1-pound chicken tenders

- 10 strips bacon

- 1/2 tbsp Italian seasoning

- 1/2 tbsp black pepper

- 1/2 tbsp salt

- 1 tbsp paprika

- 1 tbsp onion powder

- 1 tbsp garlic powder

- 1/3 cup light brown sugar

- 1 tbsp chili powder

Directions:

1. Preheat your wood pellet smoker to 350°F.

2. Mix seasonings

3. Sprinkle the mixture on all sides of chicken tenders

4. Wrap each chicken tender with a strip of bacon

5. Place them on the smoker and smoker for 30 minutes with the lid closed or until the chicken is cooked.

6. Serve and enjoy.

Nutrition:

Calories: 206 Cal

Fat: 7.9 g

Carbohydrates: 1.5 g

Protein: 30.3 g

Fiber: 0 g

23 Buffalo Chicken Wings

Preparation Time: 15 Minutes

Cooking Time: 25 Minutes

Servings: 6

Ingredients:

- 2 lb. chicken wings

- 1/2 cup sweet, spicy dry rub

- 2/3 cup buffalo sauce

- Celery, chopped

Directions:

1. Start your wood pellet grill.

2. Set it to 450 degrees F.

3. Sprinkle the chicken wings with the dry rub.

4. Place on the grill rack.

5. Cook for 10 minutes per side.

6. Brush with the buffalo sauce.

7. Grill for another 5 minutes.

8. Dip each wing in the buffalo sauce.

9. Sprinkle the celery on top.

Nutrition:

Calories 935

Total fat 53g

Saturated fat 15g

Protein 107g

Sodium 320mg

Preparation Time: 30 Minutes

Cooking Time: 5 Hours

Servings: 4

Ingredients:

- Eight chicken drumsticks
- 1/4 cup soy sauce
- 1 cup ketchup
- Two tablespoons rice wine vinegar
- Two tablespoons lemon juice
- Two tablespoons honey
- Two tablespoons garlic, minced
- Two tablespoons ginger, minced
- One tablespoon sweet-spicy dry rub
- Three tablespoons brown sugar

Directions:

1. Combine all the sauce fixings in a bowl.

2. Mix well.

3. Take half of the mixture, transfer to another bowl and refrigerate.

4. Add the chicken to the bowl with the remaining sauce.

5. Toss to coat evenly.

6. Cover and refrigerate for 4 hours.

7. When ready to cook, take the chicken out of the refrigerator.

8. Discard the marinade.

9. Turn on your wood pellet grill.

10. Set it to smoke.

11. Set the temperature to 225 degrees F.

12. Smoke the chicken for 3 hours.

13.   Serve the chicken with the reserved sauce.

Nutrition:

Calories 935

Total fat 53g

Saturated fat 15g

Protein 107g

Sodium 320mg

Preparation Time: 30 Minutes

Cooking Time: 4 Hours

Servings: 4

Ingredients:

- One tablespoon honey

- Four tablespoons butter

- Three tablespoons lemon juice

- One whole chicken, giblets trimmed

- Four tablespoons chicken seasoning

Directions:

1. Set your wood pellet grill to smoke.

2. Set it to 225 degrees F.

3. In a pan over low heat, increase the honey and butter. Pour in the lemon juice.

4. Add the seasoning.

5. Cook for 1 minute, stirring.

6. Add the chicken to the grill.

7. Smoke for 8 minutes.

8. Flip the chicken and brush with the honey mixture.

9. Smoke for 3 hours, brushing the sauce every 40 minutes.

10. Let rest for 5 minutes before serving.

Nutrition:

Calories 935

Total fat 53g

Saturated fat 15g

Protein 107g

Sodium 320mg

Preparation Time: 30 Minutes

Cooking Time: 2 Hours

Servings: 6

Ingredients:

- 12 chicken lollipops

- Chicken seasoning

- Ten tablespoons butter, sliced into 12 cubes

- 1 cup barbecue sauce

- 1 cup hot sauce

Directions:

1. Turn on your wood pellet grill.

2. Set it to 300 degrees F.

3. Then season, the chicken with the chicken seasoning.

4. Arrange the chicken in a baking pan.

5. Put the butter cubes on top of each chicken.

6. Cook the chicken lollipops for 2 hours, basting with the melted butter in the baking pan every 20 minutes.

7. Pour in the barbecue sauce and hot sauce over the chicken.

8. Grill for 15 minutes.

Nutrition:

Calories 935

Total fat 53g

Saturated fat 15g

Protein 107g

Sodium 320mg

Preparation Time: 30 Minutes

Cooking Time: 3 Hours

Servings: 6

Ingredients:

- One teaspoon honey

- One teaspoon soy sauce

- Two teaspoon rice vinegar

- 1/2 cup hoisin sauce

- Two teaspoon sesame oil

- One teaspoon ginger, minced

- One teaspoon garlic, minced

- One teaspoon green onion, chopped

- 1 cup hot water

- 2 lb. chicken wings

Directions:

1. Combine all the sauce fixings in a large bowl. Mix well.

2. Transfer 1/3 of the sauce to another bowl and refrigerate.

3. Add the chicken wings to the remaining sauce.

4. Cover and refrigerate for 2 hours.

5. Turn on your wood pellet grill.

6. Set it to 300 degrees F.

7. Add the wings to a grilling basket.

8. Cook for 1 hour.

9. Heat the reserved sauce in a pan.

10.   Bring to a boil and then simmer for 10 minutes.

11.   Brush the chicken with the remaining sauce.

12.   Grill for another 10 minutes.

13.   Let rest for 5 minutes before serving.

Nutrition:

Calories 935

Total fat 53g

Saturated fat 15g

Protein 107g

Sodium 320mg

Preparation Time: 5 Minutes

Cooking Time: 25 Minutes

Servings: 4

Ingredients:

- Four chicken fillets
- Three tablespoons melted butter
- One garlic, minced
- 1-1/2 teaspoon dried Italian seasoning
- Salt and pepper to taste
- One lemon, sliced

Directions:

1. Turn on your wood pellet grill.
2. Keep the lid open while burning for 5 minutes.
3. Preheat it to 450 degrees F.

4. Add the chicken fillet on top of foil sheets.

5. In a bowl, mix the butter, garlic, seasoning, salt, and pepper.

6. Brush the chicken with this mixture.

7. Put the lemon slices on top.

8. Wrap the chicken with the foil.

9. Grill each side for 7 to 10 minutes per side.

Nutrition:

Calories 935

Total fat 53g

Saturated fat 15g

Protein 107g

Sodium 320mg

Chapter 5. Fish and seafood

Preparation Time: 5 Minutes

Cooking Time: 25 Minutes

Servings: 4

Ingredients:

- 1 cup cooked salmon, flaked
- 1/2 red bell pepper, chopped
- Two eggs, beaten
- 1/4 cup mayonnaise
- 1/2 tablespoon dry sweet rub
- 1 1/2 cups breadcrumbs
- One tablespoon mustard
- Olive oil

Directions:

1. Combine all the fixings except the olive oil in a bowl.

2. Form patties from this mixture.

3. Let sit for 15 minutes.

4. Turn on your wood pellet grill.

5. Set it to 350 degrees F.

6. Add a baking pan to the grill.

7. Drizzle a little olive oil on top of the pan.

8. Add the salmon cakes to the pan.

9. Grill each side for 3 to 4 minutes.

Nutrition:

Calories 119

Total fat 10g

Saturated fat 2g

Sodium 720mg

Preparation Time: 10 minutes

Cooking Time: 15 minutes

Servings: 4

Ingredients:

- 2 (8 ounces each) lobster tails
- 1/4 tsp old bay seasoning
- ½ tsp oregano
- 1 tsp paprika
- Juice from one lemon
- 1/4 tsp Himalayan salt
- 1/4 tsp freshly ground black pepper
- 1/4 tsp onion powder
- 2 tbsp freshly chopped parsley
- ¼ cup melted butter

Directions:

1. Slice the tail in the middle with a kitchen shear. Pull the shell apart slightly and run your hand through the meat to separate the meat partially

2. Combine the seasonings

3. Drizzle lobster tail with lemon juice and season generously with the seasoning mixture.

4. Preheat your wood pellet smoker to 450°F, using apple wood pellets.

5. Place the lobster tail directly on the grill grate, meat side down. Cook for about 15 minutes.

6. The tails must be pulled off and it must cool down for a few minutes

7.   Drizzle melted butter over the tails.

8.   Serve and garnish with fresh chopped parsley.

Nutrition:

Calories: 146 Cal

Fat: 11.7 g

Carbohydrates: 2.1 g

Protein: 9.3 g

Fiber: 0.8 g

Preparation Time: 10 minutes

Cooking Time: 3o minutes

Servings: 4

Ingredients:

- 1-pound fresh halibut filet (cut into 4 equal sizes)
- 1 tbsp fresh lemon juice
- 2 garlic cloves (minced)
- 2 tsp soy sauce
- ½ tsp ground black pepper
- ½ tsp onion powder
- 2 tbsp honey
- ½ tsp oregano
- 1 tsp dried basil
- 2 tbsp butter (melted)

- Maple syrup for serving

Directions:

1. Combine the lemon juice, honey, soy sauce, onion powder, oregano, dried basil, pepper and garlic.

2. Brush the halibut filets generously with the filet the mixture. Wrap the filets with aluminum foil and refrigerate for 4 hours.

3. Remove the filets from the refrigerator and let them sit for about 2 hours, or until they are at room temperature.

4. Activate your wood pellet grill on smoke, leaving the lid opened for 5 minutes or until fire starts.

5. The lid must not be opened for it to be preheated and reach 275°F 15 minutes, using fruit wood pellets.

6. Place the halibut filets directly on the grill grate and smoke for 30 minutes

7. Remove the filets from the grill and let them rest for 10 minutes.

8. Serve and top with maple syrup to taste

9. Nutrition:

Calories: 180 Cal

Fat: 6.3 g

Carbohydrates: 10 g

Protein: 20.6 g

Fiber: 0.3 g

Preparation Time: 10 minutes

Cooking Time: 4o minutes

Servings: 8

Ingredients:

- 2 pounds salmon (cut into fillets)

- 1/2 cup low sodium soy sauce

- 2 garlic cloves (grated)

- 4 tbsp olive oil

- 2 tbsp honey

- 1 tsp ground black pepper

- ½ tsp smoked paprika

- ½ tsp Italian seasoning

- 2 tbsp chopped green onion

Directions:

1. Incorporate pepper, paprika, Italian seasoning, garlic, soy sauce and olive oil. Add the salmon fillets and toss to combine. Cover the bowl and refrigerate for 1 hour.

2. Remove the fillets from the marinade and let it sit for about 2 hours, or until it is at room temperature.

3. Start the wood pellet on smoke, leaving the lid opened for 5 minutes, or until fire starts.

4. Keep lid unopened and preheat grill to a temperature 350°F for 15 minutes.

5. Do not open lid for 4 minutes or until cooked

6. Flip the fillets and cook for additional 25 minutes or until the fish is flaky.

7. Remove the fillets from heat and let it sit for a few minutes.

8. Serve warm and garnish with chopped green onion.

Nutrition:

Calories: 317 Cal

Fat: 18.8 g

Carbohydrates: 8.3 g

Protein: 30.6 g

Fiber: 0.4 g

33 Barbeque Shrimp

Preparation Time: 20 minutes

Cooking Time: 8 minutes

Servings: 6

Ingredients:

- 2-pound raw shrimp (peeled and deveined)
- ¼ cup extra virgin olive oil
- ½ tsp paprika
- ½ tsp red pepper flakes
- 2 garlic cloves (minced)
- 1 tsp cumin
- 1 lemon (juiced)
- 1 tsp kosher salt
- 1 tbsp chili paste

- Bamboo or wooden skewers (soaked for 30 minutes, at least)

Directions:

1. Combine the pepper flakes, cumin, lemon, salt, chili, paprika, garlic and olive oil. Add the shrimp and toss to combine.

2. Transfer the shrimp and marinade into a zip-lock bag and refrigerate for 4 hours.

3. Let shrimp rest in room temperature after pulling it out from marinade

4. Start your grill on smoke, leaving the lid opened for 5 minutes, or until fire starts. Use hickory wood pellet.

5. Keep lid unopened and preheat the grill to "high" for 15 minutes.

6. Thread shrimps onto skewers and arrange the skewers on the grill grate.

7. Smoke shrimps for 8 minutes, 4 minutes per side.

8. Serve and enjoy.

Nutrition:

Calories: 267 Cal

Fat: 11.6 g

Carbohydrates: 4.9 g

Protein: 34.9 g

Fiber: 0.4 g

Preparation Time: 5 minutes

Cooking Time: 4 minutes

Servings: 4

Ingredients:

- 4 (6 ounce each) tuna steaks (1 inch thick)
- 1 lemon (juiced)
- 1 clove garlic (minced)
- 1 tsp chili
- 2 tbsp extra virgin olive oil
- 1 cup white wine
- 3 tbsp brown sugar
- 1 tsp rosemary

Directions:

1. Combine lemon, chili, white wine, sugar, rosemary, olive oil and garlic. Add the tuna steaks and toss to combine.

2. Transfer the tuna and marinade to a zip-lock bag. Refrigerate for 3 hours.

3. Remove the tuna steaks from the marinade and let them rest for about 1 hour

4. Start your grill on smoke, leaving the lid opened for 5 minutes, or until fire starts.

5. Do not open lid to preheat until 15 minutes to the setting "HIGH"

6. Grease the grill grate with oil and place the tuna on the grill

grate. Grill tuna steaks for 4 minutes, 2 minutes per side.

7. Remove the tuna from the grill and let them rest for a few minutes.

Nutrition:

Calories: 137 Cal

Fat: 17.8 g

Carbohydrates: 10.2 g

Protein: 51.2 g

Fiber: 0.6 g

Chapter 6. Vegetable

Preparation Time: 30 Minutes

Cooking Time: 20 Minutes

Servings: 4

Ingredients:

- 4 cups kale leaves

- Olive oil

- Salt to taste

Directions:

1. Drizzle kale with oil and sprinkle it with salt.

2. Set the Traeger wood pellet grill to 250 degrees F.

3. Preheat it for 15 minutes while the lid is closed.

4. Add the kale leaves to a baking pan.

5. Place the pan on the grill.

6. Cook the kale for 20 minutes or until crispy.

Nutrition:

Calories 118

Total fat 7.6g

Total carbs 10.8g

Protein 5.4g,

Sugars 3.7g

Fiber 2.5g,

Sodium 3500mg

Potassium 536mg

Preparation Time: 30 Minutes

Cooking Time: 40 Minutes

Servings: 4

Ingredients:

- Three sweet potatoes, sliced into strips

- Four tablespoons olive oil

- Two tablespoons fresh rosemary, chopped

- Salt and pepper to taste

Directions:

1. Set the Traeger wood pellet grill to 450 degrees F.

2. Preheat it for 10 minutes.

3. Spread the sweet potato strips in the baking pan.

4. Toss in olive oil and sprinkle with rosemary, salt, and pepper.

5. Cook for 15 minutes.

6. Flip and cook for another 15 minutes.

7. Flip and cook for ten more minutes.

Nutrition:

Calories 118

Total fat 7.6g

Total carbs 10.8g

Protein 5.4g

Sugars 3.7g

Fiber 2.5g,

Sodium 3500mg

Potassium 536mg

37 Potato Fries with Chipotle Peppers

Preparation Time: 30 Minutes

Cooking Time: 30 Minutes

Servings: 4

Ingredients:

- Four potatoes, sliced into strips
- Three tablespoons olive oil
- Salt and pepper to taste
- 1 cup mayonnaise
- Two chipotle peppers in adobo sauce
- Two tablespoons lime juice

Directions:

1. Set the Traeger wood pellet grill to high.
2. Preheat it for 15 minutes while the lid is closed.

3. Coat the potato strips with oil.

4. Sprinkle with salt and pepper.

5. Put a baking pan on the grate.

6. Transfer potato strips to the pan.

7. Cook potatoes until crispy.

8. Mix the remaining ingredients.

9. Pulse in a food processor until pureed.

10. Serve potato fries with chipotle dip.

Nutrition:

Calories 118

Total fat 7.6g

Total carbs 10.8g

Protein 5.4g

Sugars 3.7g

Fiber 2.5g,

Sodium 3500mg

Potassium 536mg

38 Grilled Zucchini

Preparation Time: 30 Minutes

Cooking Time: 10 Minutes

Servings: 4

Ingredients:

- Four zucchinis, sliced into strips
- One tablespoon sherry vinegar
- Two tablespoons olive oil
- Salt and pepper to taste
- Two fresh thyme, chopped

Directions:

1. Place the zucchini strips in a bowl.
2. Mix the remaining fixings and pour them into the zucchini.
3. Coat evenly.

4. Set the Traeger wood pellet grill to 350 degrees F.

5. Preheat for 15 minutes while the lid is closed.

6. Place the zucchini on the grill.

7. Cook for 3 minutes per side.

Nutrition:

Calories 118

Total fat 7.6g

Total carbs 10.8g

Protein 5.4g

Sugars 3.7g

Fiber 2.5g,

Sodium 3500mg

Potassium 536mg

Preparation Time: 1 Hour and 15 Minutes

Cooking Time: 40 Minutes

Servings: 4

Ingredients:

- 2 lb. potatoes
- Two tablespoons olive oil
- 2 cups mayonnaise
- One tablespoon white wine vinegar
- One tablespoon dry mustard
- 1/2 onion, chopped
- Two celery stalks, chopped
- Salt and pepper to taste

Directions:

1. Coat the potatoes with oil.

2. Smoke the potatoes in the Traeger wood pellet grill at 180 degrees F for 20 minutes.

3. Increase temperature to 450 degrees F and cook for 20 more minutes.

4. Transfer to a bowl and let cool.

5. Peel potatoes.

6. Slice into cubes.

7. Refrigerate for 30 minutes.

8. Stir in the rest of the ingredients.

Nutrition:

Calories 118

Total fat 7.6g

Total carbs 10.8g

Protein 5.4g

Sugars 3.7g

Fiber 2.5g,

Sodium 3500mg

Potassium 536mg

Preparation Time: 15 Minutes

Cooking Time: 15 Minutes

Servings: 8

Ingredients:

- Eight mushroom caps
- 1/2 cup Parmesan cheese, grated
- 1/2 teaspoon garlic salt
- 1/4 cup mayonnaise
- Pinch paprika
- Hot sauce

Directions:

1. Place mushroom caps in a baking pan.
2. Mix the remaining ingredients in a bowl.
3. Scoop the mixture onto the mushroom.
4. Place the baking pan on the grill.

5. Cook in the Traeger wood pellet grill at 350 degrees F for 15 minutes while the lid is closed.

Nutrition:

Calories 118

Total fat 7.6g

Total carbs 10.8g

Protein 5.4g

Sugars 3.7g

Fiber 2.5g,

Sodium 3500mg

Potassium 536mg

41 Roasted Spicy Tomatoes

Preparation Time: 30 Minutes

Cooking Time: 1 Hour and 30 Minutes

Servings: 4

Ingredients:

- 2 lb. large tomatoes, sliced in half

- Olive oil

- Two tablespoons garlic, chopped

- Three tablespoons parsley, chopped

- Salt and pepper to taste

- Hot pepper sauce

Directions:

1. Set the temperature to 400 degrees F.

2. Preheat it for 15 minutes while the lid is closed.

3. Add tomatoes to a baking pan.

4. Drizzle with oil and sprinkle with garlic, parsley, salt, and pepper.

5. Roast for 1 hour and 30 minutes.

6. Drizzle with hot pepper sauce and serve.

Nutrition:

Calories 118

Total fat 7.6g

Total carbs 10.8g

Protein 5.4g

Sugars 3.7g

Fiber 2.5g,

Sodium 3500mg

Potassium 536mg

Chapter 7. Smoking recipe

Preparation Time: 5-7 hours

Cooking Time: 2 hours

Servings: 4

Ingredients:

- Tuna steaks, 1 oz.

- 2 c. marinade, teriyaki

- Alder wood chips soaked in water

Directions:

1. Slice tuna into thick slices of 2 inch. Place your tuna slices and marinade then set in your fridge for about 3 hours

2. After 3 hours, remove the tuna from the marinade and pat dry. Let the tuna air dry in your fridge for 2-4 hours. Preheat

your smoker to 180 degrees Fahrenheit

3. Place the Tuna on a Teflon-coated fiberglass and place them directly on your grill grates. Smoke the Tuna for about an hour until the internal temperature reaches 145 degrees Fahrenheit.

4. Remove the tuna from your grill and let them rest for 10 minutes. Serve!

Nutrition:

Calories: 249 Cal

Fat: 3 g

Carbohydrates: 33 g

Protein: 21 g

Fiber: 0 g

Preparation Time: 16 hours

Cooking Time: 8 hours

Servings: 4

Ingredients:

- 5 pound of fresh sockeye (red) salmon fillets

- For trout Brine

- 4 cups of filtered water

- 1 cup of soy sauce

- ½ a cup of pickling kosher salt

- ½ a cup of brown sugar

- 2 tablespoon of garlic powder

- 2 tablespoon of onion powder

- 1 teaspoon of cayenne pepper

Directions:

1. Combine all of the ingredients listed under trout brine in two different 1-gallon bags. Store it in your fridge. Cut up the Salmon fillets into 3-4-inch pieces. Place your salmon pieces into your 1-gallon container of trout brine and let it keep in your fridge for 8 hours.

2. Rotate the Salmon and pat them dry using a kitchen towel for 8 hours

3. Configure your pellet smoker for indirect cooking. Remove your salmon pieces of from your fridge Preheat your smoker to a temperature of 180 degrees Fahrenheit

4. Once a cold smoke at 70 degrees Fahrenheit starts smoke your fillets

5. Keep smoking it until the internal temperature reaches 145 degrees Fahrenheit.

6. Remove the Salmon from your smoker and let it rest for 10 minutes

Nutrition:

Calories: 849 Cal

Fat: 45 g

Carbohydrates: 51 g

Protein: 46 g

Fiber: 0 g

44 Smoked Up Salmon and Dungeness Crab Chowder

Preparation Time: 30 minutes

Cooking Time: 45 minutes

Servings: 6

Ingredients:

- 4 gallons of water
- 3 fresh Dungeness crabs
- 1 cup of rock salt
- 3 cups of Cold-Hot Smoked Salmon
- 3 cups of ocean clam juice
- 5 diced celery stalks
- 1 yellow diced onion
- 2 peeled and diced large sized russet potatoes
- 14 ounces of sweet corn

- 12 ounce of clam chowder dry soup mix

- 4 bacon slices crumbled and cooked

Directions:

1. Bring 4 gallons of water and rock salt to a boil. Add the Dungeness crab and boil for 20 minutes

2. Remove the crabs , let it cool and clean the crabs and pick out crab meat. Place it over high heat.

3. Add clam juice, 5 cups of water, diced potatoes, diced celery, and onion. Bring the mix to a boil as well. Add corn to the liquid and boil.

4. Whisk in the clam chowder and keep mixing everything. Simmer on low for about 15 minutes and

add the crumbled bacon. Add bacon, garnish with ½ cup flaked smoked salmon and ½ cup Dungeness crabmeat. Serve!

Nutrition:

Calories: 174 Cal

Fat: 5 g

Carbohydrates: 12 g

Protein: 8 g

Fiber: 0 g

45 Alder Wood Smoked Bony Trout

Preparation Time: 4 hours

Cooking Time: 2 hours

Servings: 4

Ingredients:

- 4 fresh boned whole trout with their skin on
- For trout Brine
- 4 cups of filtered water
- 1 cup of soy sauce
- ½ a cup of pickling kosher salt
- ½ a cup of brown sugar
- 2 tablespoon of garlic powder
- 2 tablespoon of onion powder
- 1 teaspoon of cayenne pepper

Directions:

1. Combine all of the ingredients listed under trout brine in two different 1-gallon bags.

2. Store it in your fridge.

3. Place your trout in the sealable bag with trout brine and place the bag in a shallow dish.

4. Let it refrigerate for about 2 hours, making sure to rotate it after 30 minutes.

5. Remove them from your brine and pat them dry using kitchen towels.

6. Air Dry your brine trout in your fridge uncovered for about 2 hours.

7. Preheat your smoker to a temperature of 180 degrees Fahrenheit using alder pellets.

8. The pit temperature of should be 180 degrees Fahrenheit and the cold smoke should be 70 degrees Fahrenheit.

9. Cold smoke your prepared trout for 90 minutes.

10. After 90 minutes transfer the cold smoked boned trout pellets to your smoker grill are and increase the smoker temperature to 225 degrees Fahrenheit.

11. Keep cooking until the internal temperature reaches 145 degrees Fahrenheit in the thickest parts.

12. Remove the trout from the grill and let them rest for 5 minutes.

13. Serve!

Nutrition:

Calories: 508 Cal

Fat: 23 g

Carbohydrates: 47 g

Protein: 15 g

Fiber: 0

Chapter 8. Baking recipe

Preparation Time: 5 minutes

Cooking Time: 6 minutes

Servings: 8

Ingredients:

- 1 watermelon, sliced

- Feta cheese

- Mint leaves, chopped

Directions:

1. Preheat your wood pellet grill to 450 degrees F.

2. Grill the watermelon for 3 minutes per side.

3. Slice into cubes.

4. Transfer to a bowl.

5.   Top with the cheese and mint leaves.

Nutrition:

Calories: 14 Cal

Fat: 0 g

Carbohydrates: 3 g

Protein: 0 g

Fiber: 0 g

Preparation Time: 5 minutes

Cooking Time: 10 minutes

Servings: 6

Ingredients:

- 1/2 tablespoon ground cinnamon

- 3 tablespoons brown sugar

- 3 peaches, sliced in half and pitted

- 1 tablespoon melted butter

Directions:

1. Turn on your wood pellet grill.

2. Set it to smoke.

3. Establish fire in the burn pot for 5 minutes.

4. Set it to 400 degrees F.

5.   In a bowl, mix the cinnamon and brown sugar.

6.   Coat the peaches with the butter.

7.   Grill for 6 minutes.

8.   Flip and sprinkle with the sugar mixture.

9.   Grill for 2 minutes.

Nutrition:

Calories: 98 Cal

Fat: 6 g

Carbohydrates: 12 g

Protein: 1 g

Fiber: 1 g

Preparation Time: 5 minutes

Cooking Time: 5 minutes

Servings: 4

Ingredients:

- 1 tablespoon lemon juice

- 4 tablespoons honey

- 16 strawberries

Directions:

1. Turn on your wood pellet grill.

2. Set it to 450 degrees F.

3. Thread the strawberries into skewers.

4. Brush with the honey and lemon juice.

5. Grill for 5 minutes.

Nutrition:

Calories: 53 Cal

Fat: 0 g

Carbohydrates: 12 g

Protein: 1 g

Fiber: 3 g

Chapter 9. Dessert recipe

Preparation Time: 15 Minutes

Cooking Time: 35 Minutes

Servings: 8

Ingredients:

- Pepper
- Salt
- One t. vinegar
- Two T. olive oil
- Two eggs
- One chopped onion
- One soaked slice of bread
- ½ t. cumin
- One T. chopped basil
- 1 ½ T. chopped parsley

- 2 ½ pounds ground beef

Directions:

1. Use your hands to combine everything until thoroughly combined. If needed, when forming meatballs, dip your hands into some water. Shape into 12 meatballs.

2. Add wood pellets to your smoker.

3. Preheat your smoker, with your lid closed, until it reaches 380.

4. Place the meatballs onto the grill and cook on all sides for eight minutes. Take off the grill and let sit for five minutes.

5. Serve with favorite condiments or a salad.

Nutrition:

Calories: 33

Carbs: 6g

Fat: 0g Protein: 1g

50 Greek Meatballs

Preparation Time: 10 Minutes

Cooking Time: 40 Minutes

Servings: 6

Ingredients:

- Pepper
- Salt
- Two chopped green onions
- One T. almond flour
- Two eggs
- ½ pound ground pork
- 2 ½ pound ground beef

Directions:

1. Mix all the ingredients using your hands until everything is incorporated evenly. Form mixture into meatballs until all meat is used.

2. Add wood pellets to your smoker and follow your cooker's startup procedure. Preheat your smoker, with your lid closed, until it reaches 380.

3. Brush the meatballs with olive oil and place onto the grill—Cook for ten minutes on all sides.

Nutrition:

Calories: 161

Carbs: 10g

Fat: 6g

Protein: 17g

51 Grilled Pineapple with Chocolate Sauce

Preparation Time: 10 Minutes

Cooking Time: 25 Minutes

Servings: 8

Ingredients:

- 1pineapple

- 8 oz bittersweet chocolate chips

- 1/2 cup spiced rum

- 1/2 cup whipping cream

- 2tbsp light brown sugar

Directions:

1. Preheat pellet grill to 400°F.

2. De-skin, the pineapple, then slice the pineapple into 1 in cubes.

3. In a saucepan, combine chocolate chips. When chips begin to melt, add rum to the

saucepan. Continue to stir until combined, then add a splash of the pineapple's juice.

4. Add in whipping cream and continue to stir the mixture. Once the sauce is smooth and thickening, lower heat to simmer to keep warm.

5. Thread pineapple cubes onto skewers. Sprinkle skewers with brown sugar.

6. Place skewers on the grill grate. Grill for about 5 minutes per side, or until grill marks begin to develop.

7. Remove skewers from grill and allow to rest on a plate for about 5 minutes. Serve alongside warm chocolate sauce for dipping.

Nutrition:

Calories: 112.6

Fat: 0.5 g

Cholesterol: 0

Carbohydrate: 28.8 g

Fiber: 1.6 g

Sugar: 0.1 g

Protein: 0.4 g

Preparation Time: 10 Minutes

Cooking Time: 25 Minutes

Servings: 4

Ingredients:

- 2nectarines halved and pitted
- 2tsp honey
- 4tbsp Nutella
- 4scoops vanilla ice cream
- 1/4 cup pecans, chopped
- Whipped cream, to top
- 4cherries, to top

Directions:

1. Preheat pellet grill to 400°F.
2. Slice nectarines in half and remove the pits.

3. Brush the inside (cut side) of each nectarine half with honey.

4. Place nectarines directly on the grill grate, cut side down—Cook for 5-6 minutes, or until grill marks develop.

5. Flip nectarines and cook on the other side for about 2 minutes.

6. Remove nectarines from the grill and allow it to cool.

7. Fill the pit cavity on each nectarine half with 1 tbsp Nutella.

8. Place one scoop of ice cream on top of Nutella. Top with whipped cream, cherries, and sprinkle chopped pecans. Serve and enjoy!

Nutrition:

Calories: 90

Fat: 3 g

Carbohydrate: 15g

Sugar: 13 g

Protein: 2 g

Preparation Time: 10 Minutes

Cooking Time: 35 Minutes

Servings: 4

Ingredients:

- 1/2 cup flour
- 1tbsp cornstarch
- 1/2 tsp baking powder
- 1/8 tsp baking soda
- 1/8 tsp ground cinnamon
- 1/2 tsp kosher salt
- 1/4 cup buttermilk
- 1/4 cup sugar
- 11/2 tbsp butter, melted
- 1egg
- 1/2 tsp vanilla

- Topping
- 2tbsp sugar
- 1tbsp sugar
- 1tsp ground cinnamon

Directions:

1. Preheat pellet grill to 350°F.

2. In a medium bowl, combine flour, cornstarch, baking powder, baking soda, ground cinnamon, and kosher salt. Whisk to combine.

3. In a separate bowl, combine buttermilk, sugar, melted butter, egg, and vanilla. Whisk until the egg is thoroughly combined.

4. Pour wet mixture into the flour mixture and stir. Stir just until combined, careful not to overwork the mixture.

5. Spray mini muffin tin with cooking spray.

6. Spoon 1 tbsp of donut mixture into each mini muffin hole.

7. Place the tin on the pellet grill grate and bake for about 18 minutes, or until a toothpick can come out clean.

8. Remove muffin tin from the grill and let rest for about 5 minutes.

9. In a small bowl, combine 1 tbsp sugar and 1 tsp ground cinnamon.

10. Melt 2 tbsp of butter in a glass dish. Dip each donut hole in the melted butter, then mix and toss with cinnamon sugar. Place completed donut holes on a plate to serve.

Nutrition:

Calories: 190

Fat: 17 g

Carbohydrate: 21 g

Fiber: 1 g

Sugar: 8 g

Protein: 3 g

Conclusion

So now that we have reached the end of the book, I am very optimistic that you are well acquainted with some of the finest smoker grill recipes, which will make you a pro at grilling, BBQ, and cooking in general.

Sometimes seeing so many recipes briefly can be very overwhelming. So, go through the book as and when needed and make sure to follow the instructions in the recipe thoroughly.

You have obtained every secret to cooking with a Wood Pellet Smoker-Grill, and you have tons of great recipes to try again and again. All you need to do is follow the ingredients and instructions accurately. You have many kinds of recipes, so you can try a new dish every day and test your cooking skills. Practicing will improve your ability to obtain great flavors from this smoker-grill.

When you put a smoker to the right use and use the best kind of pellets, the flavor induced is so amazing that not only you but every guest who ends up eating the food is sure to be amazed at the exceptional culinary skills which you possess. I have put in a lot of love, effort, and time into this book to make sure that every recipe is as good as I wanted it to be. Of course, like always, most recipes allow you to do a little makeshift if suppose you are missing out on some ingredients. However, to get the best results, we want you to stick to the details as closely as it is possible for you.

To start cooking, go through the process of using your Wood Pellet Smoker-Grill and understanding the benefits, so you can leverage the equipment to its fullest ability when cooking.

That way, you will be trying different methods of cooking, such as smoking, grilling, searing, and more. The instructions are simple, so you just need to follow them as they are presented.

The Wood Pellet Smoker-Grill is much easier than your traditional grills and smokers, so you do not have to feel concerned at all. Just give yourself the required initial practice to obtain a complete understanding of the functionality of this appliance. With regular practice, you will grow more confident and comfortable using the smoker-grill for cooking a variety of dishes.

So, make the most of this amazing cookbook and try these recipes so that you could take your food buds for a real ride.

I hope you enjoy cooking these recipes as much as I enjoyed jotting it down for you. I'm telling this from personal experience that once you get hooked to the BBQ style of cooking, there is no way you're going to stay away from it.

Last but not least, as we had mentioned at the very start of the book, you have to make sure that you end up buying the best kind of smokers and use the perfect pellets, or else you will lose out on getting the real authentic flavor for these perfect recipes. Tweak them a little if you so desire, but I believe they are as perfect as you would want them to be.

So, be all set to enjoy the good cooking times.

CPSIA information can be obtained
at www.ICGtesting.com
Printed in the USA
BVHW060439250321
603396BV00004B/258